The Mind at Odds

Understanding Cognitive Dissonance

Freudian Trips

Copyright Page

© 2023 by Freudian Trips

All rights reserved. No part of this book may be reproduced in any form or by any electronic or mechanical means, including information storage and retrieval systems, without permission in writing from the publisher, except by a reviewer who may quote brief passages in a review.

This book is a work of non-fiction. Unless otherwise noted, the author and the publisher make no explicit guarantees as to the accuracy of the information contained in this book and will not be held responsible for any errors or omissions.

Published by Omniterra Media Inc

First Edition

Visit the author's website at www.freudiantrips.com

Disclaimer

The views and opinions expressed in this book are those of the author(s) and do not necessarily reflect the official policy or position of any other agency, organization, employer, or company. The contents of this book are for informational and educational purposes only and are not intended to serve as professional advice, diagnosis, or treatment.

The information provided in this book is believed to be accurate and reliable as of the date of publication. However, it may include some errors or inaccuracies, and no warranty or guarantee is provided regarding the accuracy, timeliness, or applicability of the content.

Readers are encouraged to consult with professional philosophers, educators, or other qualified professionals where appropriate for personalized advice. The author(s) and publisher shall not be liable for any loss, damage, or harm caused or alleged to be caused, directly or indirectly, by the information or ideas contained, suggested, or referenced in this book.

By reading this book, the reader acknowledges and agrees that they are solely responsible for how they interpret and apply the information contained herein.

This book may also include references to other works, studies, and sources. These references are provided for further reading and exploration and do not imply endorsement or validation of the specific theories, viewpoints, or interpretations presented in those works.

Introduction: The Conflicted Mind

Imagine you're a lifelong vegetarian. You love animals, believing wholeheartedly that eating meat is wrong. But one night, at a friend's barbecue, the smell of sizzling burgers is too tempting. You take a bite, then another... and it's delicious. Suddenly, you're facing a clash of beliefs: You love animals, but you also enjoyed the taste of meat. This unsettling feeling is at the heart of something called cognitive dissonance.

Cognitive dissonance is like a mental itch. It's the uncomfortable feeling you get when you hold two ideas that don't fit together. Think of it like two puzzle pieces that just won't connect, no matter how much you try. This mismatch can sometimes be about simple things, like disliking Mondays but still being excited for the weekend. At other times, it can involve deeply held values and choices, creating genuine inner turmoil.

Understanding cognitive dissonance is like getting a backstage pass into the workings of your own mind. This theory unveils how we wrestle with contradictions, how we justify our actions, and ultimately, how we shape our own sense of who we are. In this book, we'll dive into the world of cognitive dissonance – from its fascinating origins, how it works in our brains, and how it surfaces in our everyday lives. Most importantly, we'll talk about how to overcome these mental conflicts to make choices that are in tune with our values and pave the way for personal growth.

Chapter 1: Where It All Began – Leon Festinger and the Puzzle of Human Behavior

Imagine yourself in the 1950s. Psychology is a young science, and researchers are buzzing with questions about how the human mind works. Enter Leon Festinger, a curious social psychologist determined to understand why people sometimes do things that seem to go against their own beliefs.

Festinger had a knack for cleverly designed experiments. One of his most famous studies involved a rather dull task: turning wooden pegs on a board for an hour straight. Afterwards, he asked participants to try and convince others that the task had been exciting. Some were paid a measly $1 to lie, while others received a generous $20. Surprisingly, the people who were paid only $1 actually ended up believing the task had been more enjoyable than those who got a larger amount.

Why? This was the puzzle that led to Festinger's breakthrough. People paid $20 had a clear reason for lying – the money. But the $1 group was left with a dilemma. They couldn't justify lying for such a small reward, so instead, they started changing their minds about the task to avoid feeling like they had acted against their beliefs. This mismatch – between what they thought and what they did – was the recipe for cognitive dissonance.

Festinger's findings were groundbreaking. His 1957 book, "A Theory of Cognitive Dissonance", became a psychology classic. It showed that our minds aren't just a jumble of ideas – they crave consistency. When things don't line up, we do mental gymnastics to try and restore order.

But Festinger wasn't alone in exploring this idea. Researchers like Fritz Heider explored how we perceive balance in our relationships. Others focused on how dissonance can drive us to change our opinions to justify our choices. Together, these pioneers created a solid foundation for understanding the way our minds strive for harmony, even if it means bending the truth a little.

Chapter 2: Dissonance Under the Microscope

Think of cognitive dissonance like having an annoying alarm going off in your head. It gets louder and more bothersome the longer you ignore it. So, what makes this mental alarm go off in the first place? Let's break it down into a few main types:

- **Forced Compliance: Doing Something You Don't Agree With** Imagine having to give a presentation promoting a product you don't believe in. You're going against your own opinion, and that creates dissonance. It's that feeling of "I can't believe I just said that!"

- **Belief Disconfirmation: When Reality Challenges Your Ideas** Let's say you're convinced that a particular brand of yogurt is the best. Then, you see a convincing study showing a different brand to be healthier. That misalignment between what you believed and the new information is a big dissonance alarm.

- **Decision-Making Dissonance: The "What Ifs" After a Choice** You're choosing between two job offers, each with pros and cons. After you make the choice, you may start dwelling on the positive aspects of the job you didn't take – that's dissonance rearing its head!

Dissonance in the Brain

It turns out this mental discomfort isn't just a feeling – it has a physical basis in our brains. Areas linked to emotions and conflict detection light up when we experience dissonance. It's as though our brains are sending us a signal that something doesn't add up.

The Dissonance Dance: How We Get That Alarm to Stop

That feeling of dissonance is hard to live with! Our brains are wired to want things to make sense. So we use all sorts of tricks to reduce it:

- **Change Your Belief:** Maybe you decide the yogurt study wasn't that convincing after all.
- **Change Your Behavior:** You might quit the job presenting a product you dislike.
- **Justify:** "The pay was great, so it was worth saying what I had to say."
- **Minimize Importance:** "It's just yogurt, why am I making such a big deal about it?"

The way we tackle dissonance is highly personal. Some people are adamant about sticking to their beliefs, while others are more flexible. The important thing is recognizing when these mental balancing acts are happening, because they shape our choices and the ways we see the world.

Chapter 3: Where the Rubber Hits the Road – Dissonance in Our Daily Lives

Cognitive dissonance isn't just a fancy theory in a psychology textbook. It's a hidden force that shapes our actions and relationships every single day. Let's take a look at a few areas where it often shows up:

Shopping with Dissonance

Picture this: You're convinced you need those new, expensive sneakers. But are they *really* worth the price tag? After the purchase, dissonance kicks in. To ease the discomfort, you might hype yourself up, focusing on how great the sneakers look and convince yourself they were a must-have. Companies are well aware of this, which is why marketing often focuses on making us feel good about our choices even before we buy.

Dissonance and Those Close to Us

Dissonance isn't just about how we spend money, it's also interwoven with our relationships:

- **Friendships:** Imagine your best friend starts saying things you find offensive. Dissonance sets in – you care about them but don't agree with their views. You might try to ignore it, justify their behavior, or even start to question your own values.
- **Romance:** You discover your partner has been hiding something from you. The dissonance between how you see them and their actions can be deeply unsettling.
- **Family:** Maybe your parents disapprove of your career choice. Dealing with that dissonance can create tension and force you to try and bridge the gap between what they expect and what you believe.

The Ethics of It All: When Dissonance Leads Us Astray

Dissonance even plays a role in ethical choices, from those little white lies to more serious lapses in judgment:

- **"It's just this once":** Imagine needing to borrow a small amount of money from work, promising yourself you'll pay it back. That "it's no big deal" thought eases the dissonance between knowing it's wrong and doing it anyway.
- **The Slippery Slope:** Small ethical compromises can pave the way for bigger ones. Justifying a little lie to protect someone's feelings can make it easier to tell more serious ones later on.
- **Groups and Pressure:** Being part of a group can increase dissonance, as we may do things to fit in, even when they conflict with our conscience.

Cognitive dissonance might seem messy at times, but understanding how it influences us gives us a new perspective. The next time you catch yourself justifying a questionable decision, or feeling torn between who you are and the situation you're in, ask yourself: Could dissonance be at play?

Chapter 4: Dissonance and the Wider World

Imagine cognitive dissonance as a ripple in water. It might start small, within our individual minds, but those ripples can spread far and wide, shaping our communities and even world events. Let's look at some areas where its impact is particularly dramatic:

Politics: Divided We Stand

Politics is a breeding ground for dissonance. Think about these scenarios:

- **My Candidate vs. Yours:** Your preferred candidate gets caught in a scandal. Instead of changing your support, you might dig in your heels, finding reasons to discredit the evidence – dissonance at work!
- **Echo Chambers:** We often surround ourselves with news and people who agree with us. This limits exposure to opposing views, making it easier to ignore dissonance-causing information.

- **Spread of Untruths:** Misinformation thrives on dissonance. If a conspiracy theory fits neatly into your worldview, you're less likely to question its validity, even if it lacks solid evidence.

This creates a cycle where dissonance drives polarization, making constructive conversations about important issues almost impossible.

Cults and Extremism: Trapped by Belief

Cults and extremist groups use dissonance to manipulate individuals:

- **The Hook:** They often target people when they're vulnerable, offering simple solutions to complex problems. This gives a sense of belonging and reduces dissonance about life's uncertainties.
- **Step by Step:** New members are exposed to the group's ideology gradually. Small compromises make it harder to turn back, as dissonance grows between past beliefs and full commitment to the group.
- **Breaking Away is Painful:** Leaving these groups creates enormous dissonance. It means confronting the fact that you've been manipulated and potentially losing your entire support network.

Your Health, Your Choices

Dissonance even plays a role in our healthcare choices:

- **The Smoker's Dilemma:** Smokers know the dangers, but find ways to justify the habit: "It calms me down", "My grandma smoked until she was 90".
- **Fear and Vaccines:** Conspiracy theories and fear-mongering around vaccines create dissonance for parents, leading some to make choices that endanger their children and public health.
- **Miracle Cures:** When conventional medicine doesn't have a ready answer, people may turn to unproven treatments out of desperation. Dissonance makes them grasp for something, even if the evidence is weak.

Awareness is Key

Understanding the role of dissonance helps us make sense of why people sometimes cling to ideas even when they seem harmful. It doesn't excuse dangerous behavior, but it allows us to approach these complex issues with more understanding, and maybe even a bit more compassion.

Chapter 5: Finding Your Inner Harmony – Strategies for Overcoming Dissonance

Picture your mind as a house. Cognitive dissonance is like a stubborn leak– annoying, and if ignored long enough, it can cause real damage. Luckily, there are things you can do to fix the leak and create a more harmonious mental space.

Step 1: The Dissonance Detector

Identifying dissonance is the first step to overcoming it. Start paying attention to those moments of mental discomfort. Ask yourself:

- **Feeling at Odds:** Do my actions seem out of sync with what I believe?
- **Excuses Galore:** Am I making lots of justifications for a decision or behavior?
- **Selective Attention:** Am I dismissing information that challenges my viewpoint?

Recognizing these dissonance signals will put you back in the driver's seat of your own mind.

Step 2: Think It Through

When dissonance strikes, resist the urge to justify everything away. Practice critical thinking:

- **Challenge your assumptions:** Where did this belief come from? Is it still valid?
- **Play devil's advocate:** Seriously consider the opposite viewpoint. Could there be truth to it?
- **Seek out the full picture:** Are you relying only on information that supports what you already believe? Broaden your sources.

Step 3: Action Over Avoidance

The best long-term fix for dissonance is often aligning your behavior with your beliefs. This might mean:

- **Small Changes, Big Impact:** If you're upset about the environment, start simple. Taking shorter showers or switching off lights conserves energy and helps ease that dissonance.
- **Facing Difficult Choices:** Sometimes, we need to make tough calls, like ending a friendship that's become toxic, or leaving a job that goes against our principles.
- **No Such Thing as Perfect:** Don't aim for eliminating all dissonance, that's impossible. Growth is about making conscious choices, even when they're hard.

Dissonance and Those Around Us

Understanding dissonance doesn't just help ourselves, it can make us more understanding towards others:

- **Question, Don't Condemn:** Instead of getting angry when someone expresses a view you disagree with, try to see the world through their eyes. What might be causing their dissonance?
- **Seek common ground:** Can you find shared values, even if you disagree on certain points? This creates space for less combative conversations.
- **Acceptance has limits:** Understanding dissonance doesn't mean giving up your own principles or tolerating harmful beliefs.

Overcoming dissonance is a journey, not a destination. It takes practice and a willingness to face uncomfortable truths within ourselves. But the rewards are great: inner peace, greater clarity about what matters to you, and the ability to build more genuine connections with those around you.

Conclusion: The Harmony Within Reach

As we wrap up this exploration of cognitive dissonance, let's remember a few key things:

- **Dissonance is Normal:** We all wrestle with conflicting thoughts and feelings at times. That mental disharmony is an unavoidable part of being human.
- **Awareness is Power:** Recognizing dissonance as it happens gives us a choice. We can either be at the mercy of our minds' tricks, or we can choose to confront it and grow.
- **Choices Matter:** How we resolve dissonance shapes who we are. Aligning our actions with our beliefs leads to self-respect and a clearer sense of purpose.
- **It's Not Just About You:** Understanding dissonance helps us see the world with more nuance, making space for empathy even when we disagree.

Why Bother? Because the World Needs It!

In a world overflowing with information – true and false – the ability to think critically and question even our own deeply held beliefs is more vital than ever. Overcoming cognitive dissonance helps us cut through the noise and resist the pull of tribalism and polarization that plagues our society.

A Call for Open Minds and Open Hearts

Imagine a world where people were more comfortable with a little uncertainty. A world where changing your mind based on new evidence was seen as a strength, not a weakness. A world where intense debate could coexist with respect and compassion.

Overcoming dissonance won't magically create this world, but it's a step in the right direction. It starts with each of us being brave enough to look within, challenge our assumptions, and make choices that honor our true values. As we create more harmony within ourselves, we contribute to building a more understanding and compassionate world for all.

About Freudian Trips

Welcome to Freudian Trips, your dedicated platform for diving deep into the world of psychology. We are more than just a YouTube channel or a book publisher. We are a beacon of enlightenment, making complex psychological concepts accessible and engaging for all.

Our YouTube channel is a rich repository of psychology made simple. We take the profound and often complex ideas from the world of psychology and break them down into digestible, easy-to-understand content. From the foundational theories of Freud to the cognitive insights of Piaget, we cover a broad spectrum of psychological schools and thoughts, making psychology accessible to everyone, regardless of their background or prior knowledge.

As a book publisher, we take the same approach, transforming intricate psychological theories into comprehensible narratives. Our books are not just collections of words, but vessels of wisdom that make psychology approachable and relatable. We believe that psychology should not be confined to academic circles, but should be available to all who seek to understand the human mind and behavior.

At Freudian Trips, we believe in the power of curiosity and the pursuit of knowledge. We are here to stoke the fires of your curiosity, to guide you on your intellectual journey, and to help you navigate the fascinating world of psychology.

If you are someone who is not afraid to question, to explore, and to learn, then you are in the right place. Join us on this journey of exploration, as we make psychology easy to understand, one concept at a time.

Be sure to visit our Youtube channel at:
www.freudiantrips.com/youtube

You can also visit us on the web at www.freudiantrips.com

Welcome to The Freudian Trip community. Stay curious. Stay enlightened.